Strings of Faith

MW00955181

PIANO AND VIOLIN

VIOLIN ONLY

Isaiah 12: 2

"Behold, God is my salvation; I will trust and not be afraid;
for the Lord Jehovah is my strength and my song"

This book is dedicated to
my husband, Jason, and our six beautiful children:
Emily, Gabriel, Spencer, Jacob, Dylan and Madeline.
They have taught me how to see God's love through them.

Thank you to Lisa Atwood and Michelle Murray for collaborating
with me on this project. I am grateful to them for their assistance
with the violin music notation.

I am grateful to my Savior, Jesus Christ, for His mercy and His atoning
sacrifice. I am also thankful for the peace in my heart
that I receive through His loving grace.

I Need Thee Every Hour

Arranged by
Susan W. Henry

Music by
Robert Lowry

How Great Thou Art

Arranged by
Susan W. Henry

Words by Stuart K. Hine
Music Swedish folk melody/adapt. and arr. Stuart K. Hine

Amazing Grace

Arranged by
Susan W. Henry

Music by
E.O. Excell

Be Thou My Vision

Arranged by
Susan W. Henry

Music
Irish Folk Melody

Fairest Lord Jesus

Arranged by
Susan W. Henry

Music
Silesian Folk Song

Nearer, My God, to Thee

Arranged by
Susan W. Henry

Music by
Lowell Mason

I Know That My Redeemer Lives (Variation I)

Arranged by
Susan W. Henry

Music by
Lewis D. Edwards

32

I Know That My Redeemer Lives (Variation II)

Arranged by
Susan W. Henry

Music by
Lewis D. Edwards

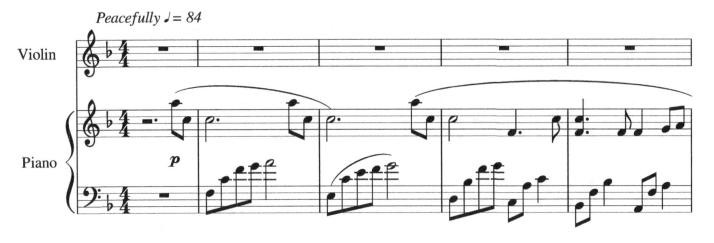

It is Well with My Soul

Arranged by
Susan W. Henry

Music by
Philip P. Bliss

Sweet Hour of Prayer

Arranged by
Susan W. Henry & Jason S. Henry

Music by
William B. Bradbury

Precious Savior, Dear Redeemer

Come Thou Fount of Every Blessing

Arranged by
Susan W. Henry

Music by
H.R. Palmer
Robert Robinson

48

Turn Your Eyes Upon Jesus

Arranged by
Susan W. Henry

Words and Music by
Helen Howarth Lemmel

Where Can I Turn for Peace?

Arranged by
Susan W. Henry

Music by
Joleen G. Meredith

Abide With Me!
There is a Green Hill Far Away

Arranged by
Susan W. Henry

Music by
William H. Monk
John H. Gower

Jesus Paid It All

Arranged by
Susan W. Henry

Music by
John T. Grape

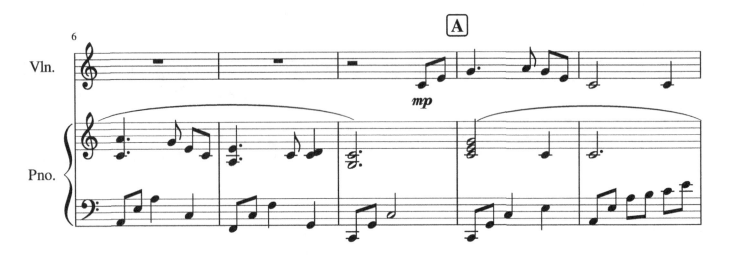

For the Beauty of the Earth

Arranged by
Susan W. Henry

Music by
Conrad Kocher

74

Come Follow Me

Arranged by
Susan W. Henry

Music by
Samuel McBurney

SECTION II

Strings of Faith and Praise
Violin Solos

Violin Only

VIOLIN
I Need Thee Every Hour

Arranged by
Susan W. Henry

Music by
Robert Lowry

81

VIOLIN
How Great Thou Art

Arranged by
Susan W. Henry

Words by Stuart K. Hine
Music Swedish folk melody/adapt. and arr. Stuart K. Hine

VIOLIN
Amazing Grace

Arranged by
Susan W. Henry

Music by
E.O. Excell

VIOLIN
Be Thou My Vision

Arranged by
Susan W, Henry

Music
Irish Folk Melody

VIOLIN
Fairest Lord Jesus

Arranged by
Susan W. Henry

Music
Silesian Folk Song

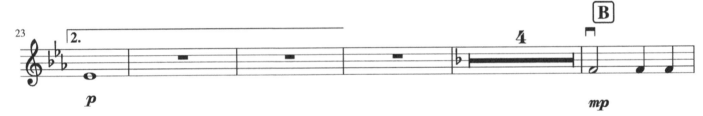

VIOLIN
Nearer, My God, to Thee

Arranged by
Susan W. Henry

Music by
Lowell Mason

VIOLIN
I Know That My Redeemer Lives (Variation I)

Arranged by
Susan W. Henry

Music by
Lewis D. Edwards

VIOLIN
I Know That My Redeemer Lives (Variation II)

Arranged by
Susan W. Henry

Music by
Lewis D. Edward

VIOLIN
It is Well with My Soul

Music by
Philip P. Bliss

Arranged by
Susan W. Henry

VIOLIN
Sweet Hour of Prayer

Arranged by
Susan W. Henry & Jason S. Henry

Music by
William B. Bradbury

91

VIOLIN
Precious Savior, Dear Redeemer
Come Thou Fount of Every Blessing

Arranged by
Susan W. Henry

Music by
H.R. Palmer
Robert Robinson

92

VIOLIN
Turn Your Eyes Upon Jesus

Arranged by
Susan W. Henry

Words and Music by
Helen Howarth Lemmel

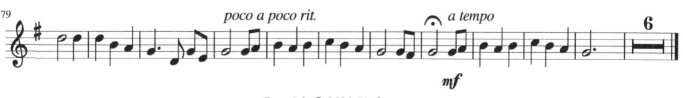

VIOLIN
Where Can I Turn For Peace?

Arranged by
Susan W. Henry

Music by
Joleen G. Meredith

VIOLIN
Abide With Me
There is a Green Hill Far Away

Arranged by
Susan W. Henry

Music by
William H. Monk
John H. Gower

VIOLIN
Jesus Paid It All

Arranged by
Susan W. Henry

Music by
John T. Grape

VIOLIN
For the Beauty of the Earth

Arranged by
Susan W. Henry

Music by
Conrad Kocher

VIOLIN
Come Follow Me

Arranged by
Susan W. Henry

Music by
Samuel McBurney